PRAYERS
of
Peace

Contributing Writers

Nancy Parker Brummett

Lain Ehmann

Marie D. Jones

Publications International, Ltd.

Cover Photo: Photodisc

Contributing Writers

Nancy Parker Brummett is a freelance writer, columnist, and the author of four books who lives in Colorado Springs, CO. Leading women closer to the heart of God is the hallmark of her speaking and writing ministries. To learn more about her life and work, visit www.nancyparkerbrummett.com.

Lain Ehmann is a Massachusetts-based writer and mom to three.

Marie D. Jones is the author of several best-selling nonfiction books and a contributing author to numerous inspirational books, including *Echoes of Love: Sisters, Mother, Grandmother, Friends, Graduation, Wedding; Mother's Daily Prayer Book;* and *When You Lose Someone You Love: God Will Comfort You.* She can be reached at www.mariedjones.com.

Acknowledgments

GOD'S PEACE

Oh, to find the peace that passes all understanding. The drama of today's average life is enough to make us crazy and bring us to our knees, crying out for peace. Yet too many times we fail to realize that we have access to the kind of peace that no challenge— no matter how big and insurmountable it might seem—can shatter. We want peace that is deep and everlasting, because it comes from the greatest source of peace there is: the loving heart of God.

Peace is not elusive. No matter how many wars we fight and conflicts we face, we forget that peace is something no one can take away from us, because it lives within us where we are touched by God. We don't always take the time to slow down and ask prayerfully for the quiet strength and wisdom that God's peace provides. Yet when we do, we are made strong in a way that nothing else can, and our troubles suddenly seem so much less dramatic. Stress melts away, cares take a hike, and we feel a sense of connectedness to a higher source of pure calm. God's peace never fails, even when our lives seem to be at war. We need to simply stop, pray, and become quiet—moving beyond our whirling minds and the endless, meaningless chatter—and let that peace fill us with the assurance that all is taken care of, all is as it should be. Only then can we know that we are right where we need to be.

Lord, bring peace to my heart and rest to my soul. These trying times leave me anxious and worried for my future and for those I love. I am struggling to find a sense of inner calm and ask for the peace that passes all understanding, the peace your love and grace can bring. I ask this not just for me but also for all those who long for calm in the storms of life. Peace be to us all. Amen.

And he said to the woman,
"Your faith has saved you; go in peace."
—Luke 7:50

O Lord, sometimes I wonder if you look down on me during the day and just shake your head at how scattered I am! As I'm pulled in one direction after the next, my life must look anything but peaceful to you. I confess that I sometimes lose the inner peace you graciously granted me when first I believed! Restore that peace in my heart, Lord, and let others see in my life the peace that could only have come from you.

＊ ＊

Heavenly Father, let me carry your peace inside me today and use it as an anchor against the tumult of my daily life. It's so easy to get lost in my routines and my to-do list. The day's demands threaten to blow me off-course, but the knowledge of your strength and omnipotence can serve as a touch point, bringing me back to serenity again and again. Help me remember that peace is only a heartbeat away, whatever my outward circumstances. Amen.

＊ ＊

God grant me a peace that is steadfast and true, a peace that never fails me no matter what is

going on in my world. Give to me a soft place
to fall and a shelter in which my heart and soul
can stay dry from the rain. Your peace gives
me hope, faith, and strength and allows me to
be strong for others who may need me. Make
me an instrument of your peace so that even as
I help myself, I can help everyone else around
me. Thank you, God.

*And he shall stand and feed his flock in the
strength of the Lord, in the majesty of the name of
the Lord his God. And they shall be secure, for now
he shall be great to the ends of the earth; and he
shall be the one of peace.*
—Micah 5:4–5

Lord, we often think of peace as something
that comes when we're ready, when our hands
are folded and our minds quiet. But your love

and presence are in all things of this world, the loud and the quiet, the raging river as well as the silent pond. You are everywhere, and it is as easy to hear you on a bustling city street as it is in the isolated silence of a redwood forest. Please remind me that I can find your peace anywhere if my eyes are open and my heart is willing. Amen.

Lord Jesus, your peace is so far from me today. I feel separated, with all my calm leaking from the broken places. I have no patience, even for those whom I love the most. Please lay your hand upon me, lending me some of your strength and stillness, so I may pass it on to others in my life. Heal my worry, still my unrest, so that I may be filled only with thoughts of your goodness and might. Amen.

O Lord, you are so good to me. What a gift it is that when I first bow my head to ask you to quiet my spirit and give me peace, you are already at work doing just that. Somehow, knowing I am in your presence, the issues and situations that seemed so difficult just a short time ago lose importance—especially when seen in the light of the peace you always have to offer. Thank you, Lord, that I can come to you in such a frazzled state and lift my head after praying, restored by your peace. You are so good.

To set the mind on the flesh is death, but to set the mind on the Spirit is life and peace.
—Romans 8:6

I celebrate today the peace of God within, a peace that is with me through all my days and never lets me down. God, your peace is my cornerstone, upon which I build the foundation of my life. In your peace, I spread peace to my family and friends, and to my community, for this indeed is a world that needs more peace. Blessed am I to have found that peace in you, God.

Peace I leave with you; my peace I give to you. I do not give to you as the world gives. Do not let your hearts be troubled, and do not let them be afraid.
—John 14:27

God, when all else fails, I know that I can count on you to give me rest and help me find peace. I am grateful to know that no matter what is going on in my life, I have someone who understands and who I can lean on. Sometimes I forget, and I lash out in anger or frustration at those I love, but you forever remind me that I only need to go within to find a place where mercy and love and peace await, and my anger and frustration disappear. Thanks be to you, God.

The Lord bless you and keep you;
the Lord make his face to shine upon you,
and be gracious to you; the Lord lift up his
countenance upon you, and give you peace.
—Numbers 6:24–26

Almighty God, how blessed we are that when you chose to send your Son to earth it was not as the prince of power and domination, but as the Prince of Peace. You knew we would need his peace both as nations populating the earth and in the innermost places of our hearts. Hear our voices lifted up in gratitude, O God! We are a people who could not survive without the

Prince of Peace in our lives. Thank you for your indescribable gift.

～～

For a child has been born for us, a son given to us . . . and he is named Wonderful Counselor, Mighty God, Everlasting Father, Prince of Peace.
—Isaiah 9:6

～～

Heavenly Father, thank you for the centered-ness you bring to my life. Even when every external thing is in an uproar, I can still come back to that still, small place and feel your Holy Spirit. I know you are with me always and that I am your beloved. I can rest in your presence in complete peace, knowing you will protect and shelter me. Thank you for your love that never fails. Amen.

～～

Lord, make me an instrument of thy peace;
where there is hatred, let me sow love;
where there is injury, pardon;
where there is doubt, faith;
where there is despair, hope;
where there is darkness, light;
and where there is sadness, joy.
O Divine Master, grant that I may not so much
seek to be consoled as to console; to be understood,
as to understand; to be loved, as to love; for it is in
giving that we receive, it is in pardoning that we
are pardoned, and it is in dying that we are born
to eternal life.
Amen.

—St. Francis of Assisi

Lord, we stand on your promises, but when it comes to your promise that your peace is with us, we sometimes stand confused. Where is your peace when young soldiers are killed in war? Where is your peace in the middle of the night when a sick child cannot be comforted? Where is your peace when a marriage is irretrievably broken? Yet even when we cannot see your peace, Lord, we know it is there because of your promise. We can find it in these and all circumstances when we come to you humbly and ask you for it. Thank you for your unfailing promise of peace. Amen.

Lord, help me quiet the noise of life long enough to find in that sacred silence a peace that knows no end. With all the clutter of daily life, I need all the solitude I can get to renew and refresh my spirit after a long, busy day. Your peace is the center I can return to time and again, a place I can rest awhile and let the concerns and worries melt away. Guide me to this place of peace within me now. Amen.

Lord Jesus, I so want to walk in your footsteps, being a beacon of love, light, and hope for this broken world. I long to fulfill your plan for me, to walk the path you have set out for me. Let me share the secret of my inner peace with all who see me by acting as you would act and loving as you would love, each and every day of my life. Amen.

Therefore I tell you, do not worry about your life, what you will eat, or about your body, what you will wear. For life is more than food, and the body more than clothing. Consider the ravens: they neither sow nor reap, they have neither storehouse nor barn, and yet God feeds them.
—Luke 12:22–24

Lord, so often my mind knows a situation will work out for good, but my heart is full of fear. Or my heart believes, but my mind races through the night with all the "what ifs" and "shoulds" that so often direct my steps. I need your peace, Lord, in both my heart and my mind. May your peace be pervasive in me, so that my first response to any situation will come from a place of peace, not a place of panic. Thank you, Lord.

And the peace of God, which surpasses all understanding, will guard your hearts and your minds in Christ Jesus.
—Philippians 4:7

You calmed the stormy waters, dear God, and quieted the thunderous skies. I ask you to calm the stormy waters for me as I struggle with the challenges I face. I know that with the peace you provide, I can face any obstacle and get

through any trial or tribulation before me. In
the stillness within, you wait for me, always
present, always ready to bring me safely back
home as a lighthouse guides a ship through
the cold, dark fog to the comfort of the shore.
Thank you for calming my storms, God.

❮❯

Our steps are made firm by the Lord,
when he delights in our way;
though we stumble, we shall not fall headlong,
for the Lord holds us by the hand.
—Psalm 37:23–24

❮❯

Praise the Lord! I am on the path of righteousness, and I will not stray. Nothing can separate
me from you, for nothing else brings me the
deep tranquility of the soul that I crave, nothing except your guiding love. You are my alpha
and my omega, and I am complete in you.

With your power, I can handle all of life's difficulties and problems, for with you all things are possible. I am at peace in your love. Amen.

~ ~

Creator God, what an amusing creature you made when you created the duck! As relaxing as it may be to watch him glide across the surface of a still, glassy pond on a summer's evening, we know he's paddling madly under the surface of the water. He's also always looking for little fish or bugs to eat, and while we're entertained when he puts his head under water and waves his tail in the air, he's really diving for survival! Is that how you see us? Calm on the surface, but paddling madly underneath— with the occasional dive for survival? All your creatures need your constant provision and care, O God. Calm our ruffled feathers, and give us your peace. Amen.

~ ~

O Lord, how amazing that just a small amount of peace, when carefully tended, can turn into pure contentment and joy. Today, Lord, make me aware of places I can plant seeds of peace in the lives of others. Could it be as simple as a gentle reply to a statement made in anger or making time to sit and listen to a troubled friend when I'd rather go home? Show me these opportunities, Lord. For I know that if I plant even the smallest seed of peace, you can nurture it to create a more peaceful world. To you be the glory! Amen.

Father, I am at war with myself over so many things. I would like to call a truce and find peace inside. Help me see that life is not black or white, right or wrong, and that sometimes just taking a different perspective is all that is needed to stop the battle within. I long to understand the peace that you promise and to cast it out into my world as a light that goes before me, making smooth my path. Father, help me lay down my arms and find peace within. Amen.

⤜ ⤐

I offer you peace.
I offer you love.
I offer you friendship.
I see your beauty.
I hear your need.
I feel your feelings.
My wisdom flows from the highest source.
I salute that source in you.
Let us work together
for unity and peace.
—Mahatma Gandhi

⤜ ⤐

Holy God, be with me today. I am entering a battlefield, and I am girding myself with your armor. I have a war against evil to fight, and though the enemy is strong, I know that righteousness will prevail. I go forth in complete peace knowing that you are in control, that I am in your care and have nothing to fear. I need no other protection than you, for you are with me today, tomorrow, and always. Amen.

For he will hide me in his shelter in the day of trouble; he will conceal me under the cover of his tent; he will set me high on a rock. Now my head is lifted up above my enemies all around me, and I will offer in his tent sacrifices with shouts of joy; I will sing and make melody to the Lord.
—Psalm 27:5–6

I sing out in praise today, for the Lord has made me whole. My life is filled with peace and balance, and harmony is the order of my day. My life was not always like this. I once took on way more than I should have, and it wore me down. But in God's love I now stand restored and at peace with whatever each new day brings. I know in my heart that I can handle anything as long as I am connected to the source that is my God. It is a source from which I can find all the highest and best blessings life has to offer. It is a source of pure peace.

God is faithful, and he will not let you be tested beyond your strength, but with the testing he will also provide the way out so that you may be able to endure it.
—1 Corinthians 10:13

Lord, is peace possible when my life is filled with activities, responsibilities, and worries? I wish I had time to sit and just be with you—

listening for your quiet voice amidst the tumult. Instead, I am caught up in the everyday, and I fear I'm moving farther from you. Please show me the way back to you, to your Word and your will for me. I know that the only way to find you is to seek you and that you will always find me. Amen.

The Lord is near to all who call on him,
to all who call on him in truth.
He fulfills the desire of all who fear him;
he also hears their cry, and saves them.
—Psalm 145:18–19

Lord, I know I should be feeling your peace right now, but it's just not happening. I need for you to examine my motives, my ambitions, my feelings and fears. Show me how this lack of peace is my own doing, because I know it is.

Help me to get out of my own way, Lord, so I can return to the peaceful place you desire for my soul. Thank you in advance for answering my cry for peace. I love you, Lord. Amen.

⤚ ⤙

Heavenly Father, accept my thanksgiving for the wonderful life you have given me. My family is healthy, my work is fulfilling, and I feel a deep sense of peace that I have not felt for a long time. I am so grateful to you for continuously proving to me that your will is always better than mine and that your point of view is much bigger and broader than the narrow perceptions of my little life. In gratitude I live each day knowing that there is peace in my life when I look beyond the surface of things to where you are: always present, always there. Amen.

⤚ ⤙

Lord, in the midst of the least peaceful situation imaginable, I want to reflect your peace. I ask you to open my heart so that I can feel your peace in the midst of chaos and confusion. And once I find it, Lord, please use your holy power to enable your peace to shine through me into the lives of others. I want to be a reflection of the kind of calm and peace that can only come from you. Use me, Lord. In the midst of chaos, use me.

Ask, and it will be given you;
search, and you will find;
knock, and the door will be opened for you.
For everyone who asks receives,
and everyone who searches finds,
and for everyone who knocks,
the door will be opened.
—Matthew 7:7–8

Holy God, may your peace visit our house-
hold. May you be with us when we rise, helping us set our schedules for the day. May you
be with us each minute as we go through our
routines. May you be with us as we sit down to
eat together, and may you be with us as we lay
down to sleep at night. May each member of
our family acknowledge your presence, feel your
loving hand, and rest in your peace. Amen.

Quietly, calmly, Lord, you move in my life.
Unseen yet always present, your love is a pow-
erful force I can rely on when I feel alone and
unsettled. Swiftly, surely, Lord, you work for
my good. Always you have my best interests
in mind, and your timing is always the perfect
timing for that goodness to show up in my life.
Strongly, securely I rest in your profound peace,
a place I can always go to when I need to get
away from the noise and the bustle. Sweetly,
gently, you remind me each night when I lay

down to sleep that you are watching over me and all is well in my world.

＊ ＊

Lord, I'm surrounded by a few people who are struggling through each day because, night after night, sleep eludes them. No amount of warm milk brings slumber. Even doses of sleep-inducing drugs fail to give them the blessed relief they need. Send your peaceful rest to these people, Lord. Gently close their eyes with your compassionate touch and reassure them that you who never sleeps are watching over them through the night. We ask this in your precious name. Amen.

＊ ＊

Heavenly Father, please bring peace to the relationships in my life. Some of the toughest challenges I have as a Christian involve my relationships with others. Even though we are brothers and sisters in Christ, we struggle to love each other and to treat each other with patience and loving kindness. Today, please bless me with an extra dose of inner calm, that I might retain my composure and remember your laws as I am dealing with others. I long to do what is right, and I know that with your help, I can keep your commandment to love others. I ask in Jesus' name, Amen.

I will both lie down and sleep in peace; for you alone, O Lord, make me lie down in safety.
—Psalm 4:8

God, bring peace to the rough places in the world. Bring hope to the hearts that have grown cold and love to the souls that know only violence and despair. Bring wisdom and understanding to those who see around them

only chaos. Bring comfort to those who suffer.
For you alone can show this world what true
and lasting peace is, the peace that is available
to us all if we lay down our prejudices and our
pride and take up instead the weapons of love
and tolerance. God, bring peace to the dark
places of the world, that they may know light.
Amen.

❧ ☙

For I am convinced that neither death,
nor life, nor angels, nor rulers, nor things present,
nor things to come, nor powers, nor height, nor
depth, nor anything else in all creation, will be able
to separate us from the love of God in
Christ Jesus our Lord.
—Romans 8:38–39

❧ ☙

Heavenly Father, be with those who need you
today. So many in this world have never felt the

peace that passes understanding, the calm and
serenity that comes when we turn over our lives
to your wise and loving guidance. Instead, they
live their lives alone, not realizing you are only
an arm's reach from them. For each struggling
soul, I pray that you would offer them your
boundless mercy and love, helping them come
to know you. Amen.

Lord, we hear so much in the news today about
the quest for world peace. Politicians, journal-
ists, and even pastors call for peace as if it were
an option the world can provide. But we know
that true peace can only come from you, Lord.
And so we ask that you send your unique, pow-
erful peace into the heart of every battle that is
raging—those we can see and those that are yet
to be revealed. You are the only source of lasting peace, Lord. Please bring it to our world.

Lord, how often in our search for peace do we forget to simply follow your gentle guidelines? You tell us to forgive others. If we do, we will have peace. You tell us to love our enemies. If we do, we will have peace. You tell us not to worry about what we will wear or what we will eat, but to take comfort by considering the lilies of the field and the birds in the air. If we do, we will have peace. You tell us not to worry so much about storing up stuff, but to store up treasures in heaven! If we do, we will have peace. Thank you, Lord, for showing us the way. Keep our feet on the path to peace that you planned for us. Amen.

The Lord is near to the brokenhearted,
and saves the crushed in spirit.
—Psalm 34:18

Rejoice in the Lord always; again I will say, Rejoice. Let your gentleness be known to everyone. The Lord is near. Do not worry about anything, but in everything by prayer and supplication with thanksgiving let your requests be made known to God. And the peace of God, which surpasses all understanding, will guard your hearts and your minds in Christ Jesus. Finally, beloved, whatever is true, whatever is honorable, whatever is just, whatever is pure, whatever is pleasing, whatever is commendable, if there is any excellence and if there is anything worthy of praise, think about these things. Keep on doing the things that you have learned and received and heard and seen in me, and the God of peace will be with you.
—Philippians 4:4–9

Dear God, have mercy on me. Lately, I have been living my life with so much anger and hostility, so much frustration and irritation. Help me find that calm center within, where your presence offers the peace I seek. Help me take that peace and bring it into my home, my community, and the outside world and to treat others as I would have them treat me. I need to be at peace, for only when I am peaceful within can I hope to create a peaceful place for others who share my world. Have mercy on me, God, and teach me to be at peace today.

Dear Holy Father, your quiet is so large that no sound can upset it. Your peace is so deep that no earthly worry can disturb it. You hold all the chaos of this world within you, and still you are completely calm. You are eternal and endless, and nothing I can do or say will ever upset you, forever and always the God of peace. Knowing that you are eternal and everlasting, unending and merciful, gives me comfort in my power-lessness, for you are good and just. Amen.